Jules Etienne Gigault Crisenoy, Richard Worsam Meade

Our Naval School and Naval Officers

A Glance at the Condition of the French Navy Prior to the Late

Franco-German War

Jules Etienne Gigault Crisenoy, Richard Worsam Meade

Our Naval School and Naval Officers
A Glance at the Condition of the French Navy Prior to the Late Franco-German War

ISBN/EAN: 9783744763042

Printed in Europe, USA, Canada, Australia, Japan

Cover: Foto ©Suzi / pixelio.de

More available books at **www.hansebooks.com**

OUR NAVAL SCHOOL

AND

NAVAL OFFICERS.

A GLANCE AT THE CONDITION OF THE FRENCH NAVY PRIOR TO THE LATE FRANCO-GERMAN WAR.

TRANSLATED FROM THE FRENCH OF

M. DE CRISENOY,

By Commander RICHARD W. MEADE, U. S. N.

———•◦•———

NEW YORK:

D. VAN NOSTRAND, PUBLISHER,

23 MURRAY AND 27 WARREN STREET.

1873.

PREFACE BY THE TRANSLATOR.

The following pages were translated during the moments of monotony incident to a cruise among the distant islands of the South Seas.

It occurs to me that our Gallic friends have some faults and peculiarities in their system of Naval education and government which our own Service shares in a measure with them, and I have reached the conclusion that if "done into English," and published, the remarks of M. de Crisenoy may impart to the brows of my professional brethren in authority a wrinkle or so, to the ultimate benefit of our Naval Service.

New York, *July*, 1873.

OUR

NAVAL SCHOOL AND NAVAL OFFICERS;

OR,

A GLANCE AT THE CONDITION OF THE FRENCH NAVY PRIOR TO THE LATE FRANCO-GERMAN WAR.

———————

TRANSLATED FROM THE FRENCH OF M. DE CRISENOY.

By R. W. MEADE, Commander, U. S. N.

———————

"I have often wondered," wrote the Cardinal d'Ossat to the Duke de Villeroy, Secretary of State for Foreign Affairs under Henri IV., "that our former sovereigns held our navy in so little account, possessing, as we do, so beautiful and vast a kingdom, flanked on either hand by two magnificent seas, extending nearly its entire length; and when I see here and there the petty princes of Italy, some of whom possess hardly a rood of sea coast, having each, nevertheless, his naval arsenal, and his ships of war, I feel that it is indeed a humiliation that the first Christian power of Europe has not the means of defence against four miserable galleys belonging to the Duke of Florence, nor the power to prevent him from placing a chain upon the neck of France and fetters upon its limbs."

The great diplomat who penned these lines had investigated this subject closely, and fully appreciated, on many occasions, how necessary is a Navy in its exterior relations to the policy of France.

Since this epoch both the Navy and the country have had their periods of prosperity, greatness, and glory, and this may perchance be an unfortunate moment for renewing the reproaches of the Cardinal, and, after his example, giving way to bitter regrets.

We must not, however, be too ready to despise our forefathers while regarding them in the light of our recent progress, for if we neglect nothing at this moment, in order to endow our Naval material with all the improvements of the day, let us remember in what a condition was our Fleet at the close of the First Empire, hardly fifty years since. Let us recall how uncertain was public opinion under the Restoration, as to the policy and utility of a Naval establishment. Let us not forget how often, when discussing the budget of Naval expenses, short-sighted political financiers sought to effect a dangerous economy at the expense of our Navy and our national honor.

The eye of Government is indeed fixed upon this matter, and even the country at large has made too much progress in this respect, to fear that a step backwards could or would be contemplated for a moment. But if it is permitted to those who have at heart the honor of the French flag, to view the future with confidence, while casting their eyes upon the present state of the Navy, they may certainly, without being taxed with radicalism, desire to see an important change introduced into some details, which, at this present moment, seem to specially require it. Time is in truth an indispensable auxiliary to the development of all great institutions, but our Navy has not grown old, since, like a Phœnix, it arose from the ashes of the past. The administration to whom its care has been confided, marches onward in this age of progress with a boldness which cannot be too much commended; but it finds it necessary to rest itself more than ever upon public opinion, and derive its strength from the enlightened sentiment of the country. This is more especially the case when it finds itself brought face to face with those questions pertaining to the personnel of the service, the more difficult and delicate to disentangle since they are not to be solved by mathematical calculation, and do not belong to any branch of exact science, but are purely practical.

Let us be grateful, then, to our Naval administrators, whose duties are so complex and so extended, for all that they have done and contemplate doing ; but let us not fear to frankly draw their attention to certain defective points which have evidently escaped their observation.

In the Naval service, the "personnel" and the "matériel" are to each other what the soul and the body are to the human system, both necessary to life, but having diverse needs according to their nature. While the second needs material supplies, that is to say, money ; intelligent connection and constancy in the system pursued, above all, continual and intelligent care, are absolutely necessary to the first. While the instantaneous creation of a matériel is but a question of expense, we cannot at any price instantaneously improvise a personnel. Under the Republic we had magnificent ships, guns, and munitions of war, but we had no sailors, and, above all, no *officers ;* and the Committee of Public Safety, which could and did organize armies and create skilful Generals, were absolutely incapable of creating a Fleet.

That complex and delicate structure—the ship of war —powerful as it is when controlled by the trained sea-

man, is in truth but an inert mass in unskilful and in-
experienced hands.   We had the proof of this for the
second time at the close of the Empire.   Fifteen years
had not sufficed to repair the disasters of the Reign of
Terror, while an unequal war had carried off and sadly
reunited again in the enemy's hulks, the remnant of our
naval officers and men which had escaped the proscrip-
tions of 1793, and notwithstanding the enormous sums
spent in repairing and building ships of war, notwithstanding the genius of the great Napoleon, France had
to succumb.

But all that has passed and gone ; we have had time to
heal those wounds, and no one can deny but that we
have worked hard to that end.   It may, then, seem in-
teresting and opportune to examine into these labors,
and see how far they may have been real and efficacious;
to set forth the progress made and the work accomplished,
as well as that task which, being unfinished, may, without
danger, be adjourned awhile, in view of a movement
which is transforming, with systematic rapidity, our
naval matériel to meet the economical conditions of the
day.

That which first draws our attention in the midst of
this multitude of men, bronzed by exposure to the elements—these swarthy sailors who pass their existence
their hands griping the wheel, resting on the breech of a
gun, or perched like birds on the lofty spars of their
ships,—that which, we say, requires our first attention are
their leaders, in short, their officers, with whom they
share their perils and labors, and to the intelligence and
devotion of whom they owe their safety on the great
deep—their chiefs to whom are confided these admirable
machines that we call ships, and which offer the most
complete, striking and grandest, perhaps, of human con-

ceptions. See that great hulking mass, inert in appearance, which, by its immobility, resembles a monster sleeping on the surface of the sea, and cradled in the rocking of the waves! Awaken it! Order it to move! It will obey you, and when gales arise, and nature awakes in the wild fury of the elements, it will be obedient to your will, and pursue its path without caring even for the obstacles which beset its course—the winds and the waves which howl and break around it. The English call this "a man of war," and under this novel form it is indeed a "Man" that you see—a man of iron frame and sinews of steel, lithe and agile in movement, whose blood boils in his veins, and whose soul enlightens and directs all its movements.

This soul is the Naval officer. One may understand, then, how much more vast and delicate is his task than that of any other. Isolated on the deck of his ship; separated sometimes by immense distances from the civilized world, and all the resources that it contains, it is necessary that he should find sufficient resources in himself, without resorting to any light from without. He must be able to move the numberless springs of action under his control ; above all, he must be a seaman and navigator, able to handle his ship and sails in all weather, and follow his course by the aid of the stars of heaven, determining exactly the almost imperceptible point that his vessel occupies on the surface of the globe. He must understand, besides, the mode of constructing and handling the heavy guns which fill his broadsides, and know how to handle them, even in the midst of a tempest.

He must not be ignorant either of the connection between the construction and repair of his floating dwelling, and of the powerful engines which render him the

master of the elements, any more than of Hydrography,
the Military art, and Naval administration.   And without being endowed with unusual faculties, which are the
rare apanage of some men of genius, the Naval officer
must possess a sufficiently precise knowledge of the elements of these sciences and arts to be able to make use
of them at all times.

Is there in human nature the power to fulfil similar
conditions?   The problem to be solved from this question might raise great doubt if two hundred years of
experience had not resolved it in the affirmative.   The
Naval officer can and does exist such as we have depicted
him, that is to say, *master of his situation*, and equal to
any emergency.   But it is upon two conditions.   The
first is, that we do not exact of him the entire science of
the Naval constructor or artillery officer, nor expect of
him the qualities of the accomplished administrator, and
that, leaving to the first the care of constructing ships,
to the second that of arming them, to the third that of
equipping and supplying them, we ask him solely to
utilize and animate the product of the labor of his col-
leagues in concentrating towards this sole end all his
activity and his faculties.

The second condition is, that he should receive from *a
very early age* an education conformable to the very ex-
ceptional mission he is called on to perform.   These
two principles, which we regard as essential, have been
foreseen from the formation of our Navy; the second
especially has never ceased to attract the attention of
those Ministers of Naval affairs who have at heart the
prosperity and glory of the Service.

When, after the unfortunate and perhaps premature
attempts of Charles V. and Francis I., Richelieu laid the
foundation-stone of our Naval establishment, he occu-

pied himself at once with the project of founding a Naval School destined to give France, in the future, good commanders for the vessels of his Sovereign, and fifty-five years later, in 1682, three companies of Marine Guards became definitely the nursery of this corps, which, hardly in existence as yet, under the impulse given by Colbert and De Seignelay, filled the world with the glory of its exploits.

Notwithstanding the imperfection of these first schools, we may judge of the importance attached to them from the care brought to bear upon the course of instruction and exercises, as well as in the choice of professors and instructors, some of whom have made their mark in the annals of science.

This first attempt remained stationary, and almost abandoned, for more than half a century—for the close of the reign of Louis XIV.—the regency—the niggardly administration of Cardinal Fleury, were anything but favorable to the Navy.

It made no progress whatever until after the death of this preceptor of Louis XV., when, under the influence of the scientific movement, which commenced to agitate the minds of men of that day, the sense of its importance spread little by little through our seaports.

The Duke de Choiseul has the honor of encouraging this feeling, and of availing himself of it, in order to animate with renewed life, the institution of "Les Gardes de la Marine," and to prepare in this way the elements of that brilliant naval awakening which illustrated the reign of Louis XVI. His successors imitated his example. M. de Boynes established at Havre in 1773 the first Naval School—an attempt unfortunately ephemeral, but which we have seen attempted on the same plan in our day. At last, in 1784, M. de Castries, cutting him-

self adrift from the past, established upon an entirely
new foundation, two floating schools at Brest and Toulon,
completed by two preparatory colleges at Vannes and
Alais.

Towards this epoch, the corps of Naval officers which
had been drawn for thirty years from these Naval nurser-
ies, maintained with care, encouraged and enlightened by
the labors of the Naval Academy, exercised by distant foreign cruises, and in the American war, which brought
out the genius of Suffren, d'Estaing, and La Mothe-
Piquet, had arrived at the highest degree of prosperity,
and nothing seemed able to destroy its influence and
progress in the future.

It only needed a few years more to be strengthened
and consolidated, but these years unfortunately were not
given to it.

In the space of nineteen years, we had no less than
seven Ministers of Marine ; and each one believed it his
duty to overturn the established order of his predecessor.
M. de Sartine, among others, struck with the science and
capacity of Naval officers, had effaced, in order to give
place to them, all the other specialties of the Naval service, and the result was a perturbed state of the Navy,
which had a disastrous influence on its usefulness.

Shaken, in truth, by successive shocks, this body of
men, which had rendered but recently such brilliant services to its country, saw itself sacrificed by the National
Assembly.   On one hand, the suppression of the schools ;
on the other, the guillotine, finished the work of destruction, of which the Republic and the Empire soon felt the
dismal consequences.

A day came, nevertheless, in which Napoleon I., profit-
ing by the bitter lessons of experience, comprehended
that it was not sufficient for France to be invincible on

land. This was in 1810 ; he therefore resolved to re-create a powerful Navy ; and first of all, he hastened to establish at Toulon and Brest two Naval Schools, which were not long in bearing their fruit, if we may believe the reports made in the case to Louis XVIII., six years later, when indiscreet loyalists sought to suppress the "Bona-partist Schools." *

Naval officers, however, hardly profited by the favora-ble disposition of the Emperor, and they still lacked co-hesion, scientific knowledge, and those *traditions absolutely necessary to a Navy*, when the Restoration came in to disorganize them anew by decimating its members of the Bonapartists, and founding at Angoulême a Naval Col-lege, which, after resisting for ten years the protests and outcries of all sensible Naval officers among the Admirals, finished by sinking under the weight of a defective Con-stitution. It was an abortion.

It was then, in face of the enormous void in the service, the entire lack of officers, and the elements nec-essary to fill up the register, that the Board of Admiralty under the presidency of Baron Mackau was charged with the duty of seeking a remedy to an evil which be-came worse every day ; and after some feeble attempts it resulted (1827-8) in the organization of the Naval School, such as it exists to-day, at least in all essential principles. Established in the harbor of Brest on the line-of-battle ship "Borda," this school is the first step in the career of the Naval officer. It is there that he re-ceives the principles of his peculiar and special education, of which we have presented a faint sketch.

---

* In this report, the Minister declares that of 640 young midship-men drilled in these schools all could, by their superior education, claim the highest position in their grade.

With this system, then, as a starting point, let us examine into the condition in which we find our Naval school at this moment, and let us consider the degree of perfection to which it may be carried. This is our first duty.

CHAPTER II.

It is on the 1st of October in each year that the candidates selected at the competitive examination are required to present themselves on board of the School Ship at Brest, in order to commence their Naval career.*

The age is not allowed to exceed seventeen years, a limit much inferior to that of all other technical or special schools; although it exceeds by one year the age fixed upon when the Naval School was originally organized.

In making this additional concession to the candidates, the authorities have the satisfaction at least of possessing in the French Empire a few "bachelors," more or less, and of not interrupting the studies of those who "bilge" (*i. e.* fail) at the competitive examination; but it must be borne in mind, that those who have entered the service are, at the age of twenty-three or twenty-four, only poor devils of midshipmen after all, living no better than, if as well as, ordinary College boys, and hardly having a private corner to retire to, forced at all hours of the day or night to run aloft, or to perform boat service in the ship's cutters.

"A midshipman," says a well-known note in the Regulations, "must eat and sleep when he can and where he

---

* All the departments of France have the privilege of sending a certain number of young men before the Board to compete for the privilege of entering the French Navy. The *best* only are selected.

can." His entire existence as a midshipman is summed up in these few words.

Such an excessively restless life may have its charms to offer at eighteen or twenty, but four years later it becomes dull and insupportable, and the service is not long in feeling the effects of it.

Beyond this inconvenience, however, which the authorities have sought to remedy lately, by not requiring midshipmen of the second class in certain cases to perform more than one year sea service, it is not thought that the tardy admission of the Cadets militates in any sensible degree against their education, for, thanks to the objects which constantly surround them, they quickly identify themselves with a shipboard life.

It is aloft or in the rigging that they take their recreation and exercise ; they rest their books on the immense chain cables when called to the blackboard to demonstrate some mathematical problem, and the huge main-deck bitts of the "Borda," christened by some wag the "Café de la Bitte," is the place where all conversation and discussion takes place.

All is matter of instruction, even to that certain piece of timber known as "a fore and aft carling," against which the new comers regularly break their heads as they descend to the steerage, so little is their mind penetrated by its name and the important part it performs in strengthening the vessel ; even to the hammock—the hammock, which alone of itself is worth a naval education, and in which our youngster sleeps better than in a bed of down, that is, as soon as a few tumbles on the deck have taught him to get into it properly. All this imperceptibly but rapidly transforms the landsman into the sailor.

Admiral Decrès, on a certain occasion, asked the

Emperor to establish a Naval School on shore. "Just so," said Napoleon; "I will also require the Minister of War to place the Cavalry School on board ship." "Oh, anything but that, your Majesty," said the Admiral. "Very well, then, Admiral, do you know of any means by which we can educate these lads *under* the water?" "No, Sire!" "Then," said Napoleon, "until you have found some way to do so, suppose we educate them *upon* it."

Napoleon had the true Naval instinct stronger than his Minister. Although the few advocates of Naval Schools on shore strenuously assert that it is possible in such barracks to educate our young officers thoroughly, and though, perhaps, such a system may give us here and there a few really good lieutenants, it is absolutely certain that the majority of the graduates will be worthless midshipmen, and still more worthless ensigns.

Our Naval School, then, seems to us irreproachable in its principle, and we may add that, the discipline being at once military and paternal, the actual life of the Cadet is really more comfortable there than, perhaps, anywhere else away from his home. But amusements and relaxations are completely wanting to his life, and that not in consequence of any regulation to that effect, but solely owing to a system which, since the creation of the School, has not ceased to preside over its direction, and to exercise a baleful influence upon the *morale* of the Cadets, as well as upon their instruction.

In support of this assertion, it will simply be necessary to cite the following passage, which is an extract from the report of a Special Commission, in 1834, for improving the discipline of the School, drawn up at the close of its first sitting.

In the absence of instructions to the contrary, the Port

Admiral at Brest had taken upon himself to grant to those Cadets who desired to visit their homes, a leave of absence between the periods of the scholastic terms. "After debating the matter, we have concluded," says the Commission in question, " that an absence of six weeks cannot but be injurious to the Cadets of the Second Division, in causing them to lose sight of the military lessons inculcated, thus retarding their professional education, and above all in aiding them to forget, in the entirely different customs of their homes, the subordination and discipline which is the rule on shipboard. The Commission, therefore, decides that it will be proper to suppress entirely the leave hitherto granted to the Second Division.

" Nevertheless, as a certain amount of relaxation is necessary after ten months of constant study, and as, on the other hand, it is requisite that the Professors and Instructors should receive a certain period of leave of absence, the Cadets of the Second Division, between the two scholastic terms, will not be required to study or recite. They will continue simply to be exercised in their seamanship drills, and at the great guns. They will visit all the different establishments of the dock-yard and port, and the Commander of the School Ship will take care to procure for them all the amusements that the situation admits of. At the end of the entire course, the Cadets admitted into the Navy may, upon their own request, obtain leave to pass some time at their homes before being ordered on regular sea duty." *

---

* This Commission was composed of Baron Hamelin, as President, and Messrs. De Bougainville, De Hell, De Bonnefoux and Reynaud, officers of the line, and Messrs. Lefebure de Fourcy and Fournier, Professors.

This exhibit of reasons, and the conclusions which terminate it, certainly possess, in default of any other merit, that of clearness.

And, in consequence, it has had the effect of suppressing not only the annual vacation which in all schools and colleges is looked upon as indispensable, but also the greater part of the daily leaves of absence to visit the shore.

From the 1st of October until the 1st of February, the period at which the rules relax a little in their severity, none of the Cadets go on shore at all, and the authorities do not seem to fear the destruction of the most steadfast inclinations for a sea life in thus condemning lads of sixteen and seventeen to an imprisonment on shipboard, that they would not even impose upon the oldest of our sea dogs without absolute necessity.

The effects of this are easily foreseen.

During this period the studies are generally very "*feeble*," and infractions of discipline, and fights between the several divisions, of frequent occurrence,* and thus in a measure (so far at least as the Cadets are concerned) is broken, somewhat rudely, the intolerable monotony of the long sojourn on shipboard, for the interior distractions of the "Borda" are quite as rare as the promenades on shore.

There is not, properly speaking, at this school any

---

* Since 1850 it has been found necessary to isolate more or less completely the new comers from the older Cadets, whose practical jokes upon the greenhorns had ended by violating all limits of reason. This state of things, which is not without its great inconveniences, has no other moving cause than that of ennui, and if our Naval Authorities wish to bring to a happy conclusion the means taken at this present moment to do away with "hazing," they must open some other outlet for the surplus activity of the older Cadets.

other recreation but that of seamanship exercise, and
when bad weather prevents the Cadets from going on
board the drill corvette for exercise, Thursdays and Sun-
days, they have no other resource but that of loitering
listlessly about the several decks of the School Ship, from
ten o'clock in the morning until nine at night, or else of
lounging on the desks which are ranged along the side of ·
the vessel. The new comers, it is true, devote themselves
eagerly to the perusal of the books drawn from the
library, which is open on these days; but in a little
while ennui gets the better of them too, and they can
read no longer, besides which the curious and instruc-
tive works contained in the library are not much appreciated by lads so young, and are so unfrequently at their
disposition that they are not able to read intelligently
and continuously.

When evening comes, they drag themselves listlessly
along the decks, exhausted by the great fatigue of doing
nothing, until all hands are called to stand by their hammocks, which is a joyful call for the majority of them, and
thus terminates that which is grimly termed by Regulations " a day of rest and amusement "—destined to prepare the minds of our youngsters for the labor of the en-
suing day.

We should not, however, omit to mention that there is
occasionally amusement of another description, which is
quite as exciting as it is rare. It is winter we will say,
and suddenly there comes on one of those terrific west or
nor'west gales so common in this locality, so that the poor
old craft, remembering her "good old cruising days,"
commences to roll and tumble about with surprising vigor
for her years, and a movement as regular as clockwork,
or else, heading the heavy sea and strong gale which
draws through the inlet (Goulet of Brest), she surges and

tautens her chains as if she would suddenly snap them and recover her ancient liberty.

The gale increases, and the officer of the deck, whose ordinary duties are simply confined to morning inspection or seeing hammocks piped down at night, resumes his regular post on the poop, the sailors attached to the ship are sent down on the lower deck where our Cadets are silently at their books and studies—to range and get ready the chains of the huge sheet anchors, whose flukes are just seen through the ports, as the anchors hang a' cockbill. Of course these preparations produce a perfect ferment in these young heads. If the ship would only drag! if they would only let go all the anchors! if the ship would only take the ground, or drag ashore upon some sand bank in the harbor, and so on and so on!

In the great majority of cases of this kind these hopes are not realized, the anchors hold well, and the chains too —the gale subsides, and another chance for relaxation is thus lost.

This is not always the case.

On a certain occasion, among others, at the end of February, 1848, a violent gale came on in the Road of Brest, while a hurricane of another description raged at the same time in Paris. For two days all communication between the ship and the shore was interrupted, and in one of the furious clearing up squalls of the gale, the Cadets being at their studies at the time, the ship all at once was felt to fall off in the trough of the sea, and broadside to the gale—a moment after, the loud tones of command came from the officer of the deck, to stand by both sheet anchors; the sailors jumped to their stations on the lower deck and got the Cadets out of the way of the cables on which they had been seated; then came the command "Let go!" and both chains ran out at once, while, in order that nothing should be wanting, the stern-post of the great ship gave a tremendous thump on the bottom at the same moment !

This time the hopes of all were crowned with success, and for a time there was an end to all silence and study. Even the most determined of students felt it his duty to abandon his lessons and look out the already crowded ports—for the cables had to be seen, of course, and the topic of conversation was the rapidity with which they ran out the hawse holes and the tremendous thumping of the stern-post on the bank, which, jarring the ship fore and aft, threatened in their eyes to rend her in pieces. However, at the end of an hour or so the gale subsided, and the necessary steps were taken to haul the old craft off the shoal on which she had grounded. The launch was sent to carry out an anchor, the manger boards and bulkheads were unshipped, the lower deck capstan rigged, and the messenger passed, and, O fortune unhoped for in the morning! the two divisions of Cadets were called on to work cables and haul in on hawsers for a part of the day.

It was in the midst of such occupations that, communication with the shore being re-established, the startling news was received of the revolution in Paris, and the flight of Louis Philippe.

Decidedly might the Cadets say on that day, "It never rains but it pours."

But winter has now passed away, and soon smiling spring ushers in the beautiful month of May. The heavy topmasts and lower yards, down all winter, are now sent aloft, and soon the old ship is all a-taunt once more and wears her customary look. The hill-sides and the shores of the harbor are covered with verdure and flowers ; the beautiful road of Ajot, which overlooks the bay, is revested

with its spring dress, and thronged with gay vehicles and
smiling promenaders, and during the beautiful long even-
ings, the Cadets, dolefully gathered on the poop deck or
lounging in the gun ports half hidden in the shades of twi-
light, follow with eager, wistful eyes every movement on
shore, listening to the faint music in the distance, of the
military bands, which are playing in the Place d'Armes.
Then comes Tattoo and the prolonged echoes of the heavy
gun from the fort; finally, the thousand and one whisper-
ing sounds of nature at work in the early spring repairing the breaches made during its long winter's slumber,
brought off by the night wind, while for these poor lads,
not a blade of grass to tread under foot, nor even a chance
for a moment to stretch their young legs, benumbed by
the torpor of their long confinement on the ship,—nothing
but the wooden deck, that everlasting infernal deck which
seems now to fairly burn under their feet.

Is it any great wonder, then, that these young hearts
become oppressed with sadness and discouragement, we
might even say despair in certain moments, when they
remember that they have yet to pass eighteen months of
this sort of life? These impressions, easily effaced by the
night's slumber, return to them the next day, and the
next; then, all at once the gun ports commence to look
narrow, the sides of the ship grow thicker, the decks
become more gloomy and sombre, the word "*prison*" occurs to their young minds, and it finishes by graving
itself deeply in their hearts.

Yes, to them it is indeed a prison—the ship! they seem
to have passed a century on board! Will they ever be
allowed to leave her? These ideas are but natural, for
truly at this age, a year is indeed a life-time to these
young hearts, who have reckoned, as yet, so few of them!

Nevertheless, June brings with it some relief. The

course of studies is finished, and the water is now warm enough to allow the bathing parties to resort to the beach of Ninon ; they at least enjoy a run on the sands of the bay shore, and can eat their fill of splendid Ploûgastel strawberries, which the numerous shore-boats bring to them.

Then comes the annual examinations, and the parting from the graduates, who, having finished the course, are about to be set at liberty at last. These events succeed each other in rapid succession; finally, they are embarked as sailors, on the Practice Ship, where they are to pass their two months' " vacation."

Well employed, truly, if we may credit the official report; after which, no youngster so behind-hand but that he is ready to measure his skill against the smartest topman, in furling a sail or passing a reef point. On their return to the harbor about the middle of September, the youngsters scatter like a covey of partridges, for, in the last few years, it has been discovered by those in authority, that the paternal hearthstone is not so injurious as was thought in 1834, by the gentlemen who composed the Special Commission on Discipline.

Thanks to this short vacation, the second year of study opens without actual disgust, mingled with fatigue, on the part of the Cadets, as was formerly the case ; but this impression is of short duration, and, notwithstanding the increasing interest of the course of study, the spirits of the First Division are not completely raised until the grand fête given in honor of the " C."

As is usual in most Schools and Colleges, each Cadet has a special number given him when he enters, and the " C " is the number expressed by the highest number in the School; and it also represents the number of days which must elapse before they can take their final leave of the ship. Therefore, if in the starboard division there are eighty Cadets, the last number will be 160 " C," representing 160 days ; and upon his entrance, each Cadet will have, for example, 655 days to pass on board, or 15 + 4 C.

Each morning "the equation of C," as it is called, is written in large figures on one of the blackboards, ranged along the deck, and when towards the commencement of the second year it happens that the First Division have no longer " C " days to serve, the event is celebrated by a grand dinner, that the poor " Plebes" (fisteaux) silently regard with envy through the cracks in the bulkhead.*

On the day in question, each mess table is at liberty to have a banquet prepared on shore and sent off, provided only, no wines or liquors are introduced. Therefore, when the great day arrives, huge *pâtés de foies gras*, ices, confectionery, etc., make their appearance on board, accompanied by silver-ware (more or less pure, of course, but none the less brilliant for that,) and damask table-linen of dazzling whiteness. This fête introduces, as it were, new life into the class.

From this time henceforward the course of study, so far as they are concerned, seems finished; in fact the several studies very soon come to an end, one after the other, after which follow practical exercises in navigation with the sextant, and the astronomical calculations at the Observatory, as well as the target practice with great guns, all of which carry our Cadets frequently out of the ship to their great delight. On board, a swarm of tailors may be seen every Wednesday measuring the

---

* This dinner usually took place on Shrove Tuesday. In 1863, however, it was suppressed altogether, having been found " prejudicial to discipline and injurious to the course of study."

young gentlemen for their new uniforms as Midshipmen, while scattered about here and there, are seen
swords, gold lace, embroidery, etc., all being the fore-
runner of the coming day of deliverance.

Of course, every day seems an age to those about to
depart ; but all ennui has long since fled, and the last few
months of the course are those in which the class studies
with renewed ardor, new strength being born of the
hope which wells up in all these hearts previously so
downcast. Some weeks are passed in this way. At last,
after a long and perfectly sleepless night, the happy day
of final departure dawns ! With throbbing hearts, and
some doubt at the same time as to whether they are
really awake or dreaming, the Cadets dress themselves for
the first time in their new uniforms, make a neat bundle
of their old clothes, return to the mate of the steerage the
keys of their lockers, and make final tours fore and aft
the ship, which they are about to quit at last. It is now
seven o'clock, and the shrill whistle of the boatswain's
mate is heard calling away the cutter—destined to carry
them on shore for the last time.

This time, instead of rushing as usual down the accom-
modation ladder and jumping into the boat to seize the
tiller or get the best place in the stern-sheets, the ten
midshipmen allowed to leave each day descend into the
cutter with grave and dignified demeanor, as if fully im-
pressed with a sense of their new-born importance to the
service ; nevertheless, they cast a final look at the old
ship's sides, dotted with its rows of black and white ports
—that ship which they have at length quitted for the last
time, thank God !

They are now in the cutter, but still alongside the ship.
It is the grand moment, the moment of moments, of
their lives ! " Shove off ! " says the officer of the boat.

"Shove off, sir!" repeats the bowman, using his reversed boat-hook, and suiting the action to the word. That simple command, "Shove off," penetrates the youngster's heart to its deepest core, and leaves there a souvenir which he will carry with him to the latest moment of his existence!

In face of this profound emotion, inspired by the feeling of his long-lost, but now regained liberty, the final examination which our Cadet is now required to undergo on shore disturbs him very little indeed. During his passage to the shore everything seems to wear a smiling aspect, and to have its own particular expression for him and him alone. The harbor, the docks, the slips, the streets of Brest, all are joyous, and nature seems to welcome him with open arms. He departs, carrying with him a pleasant remembrance of the Examining officers, whom he hopes some day to meet again on shipboard, and the School Ship is the only thing he quits without a sigh of regret. It has been his prison; he has been shut up there for twenty-two long weary months! Now, gentlemen in power, to speak frankly, is this the souvenir of Alma Mater that these young lads ought in justice to carry away with them into the service?

If we have been prolix on these points, it is because we feel it to be the best and only way to call attention to the ugly defects of the actual system pursued.

It is only within a few years past that the School has become sufficiently old to see its graduates reach positions of authority and influence in the service; and now that this is so, and these graduates by their rank may exact respect for their opinion, it is our duty to remind them of their former career, to the end that they should do for the Cadets of the present day what they would in former days have desired officers in power to do for them.

How often, in truth, is it the case that we find in this world men who, by dint of their own hard struggles through life, have forgotten their own early impressions, and when advanced in years endeavor to persuade themselves that all amusements militate against labor and study, while, in reality, the one is as necessary to the other, as air and light to the life of man.

> "All work and no play,
> Makes Jack a dull boy,"

says the old English proverb; and so it comes about, that, instead of earnestly seeking with intelligence to choose amusements suitable for these lads, they issue a sweeping condemnation of all amusements, with the inevitable result that we have seen. These youngsters, discouraged from the first, find their sojourn at the School, which should be a round of joyous labor, activity and emulation, transformed into a dull, unvarying routine of indolent performance of compelled duties and studies, mingled with feelings of positive disgust for the life, and a desperate ennui. The old ideas adopted at the origin of the School are not, it is true, the only obstacle to a change of system. There exists another very material one in the position of the ship herself, which, by her great draft of water, obliges her to be moored a long distance from the shore, for it is considered that if moored closer she would interfere with the other vessels in the port, and, moreover, the situation would not be so advantageous for the Cadets themselves.

Perhaps at Toulon it might be possible to find a better berth for a School Ship; but that dockyard does not seem to us as advantageous in point of locality as Brest, where the climate is more healthy, and the weather better, notwithstanding the winter gales. It seems to us, also, that the very air of Brittany and its misty atmosphere breathes the true spirit of the sea, and makes the sailor, to a far greater degree than that soft southern climate and beautifully clear sky of Toulon, which never changes its aspect, even when the fierce mistral whitens the sea with foam. Notwithstanding these difficulties, the problem is one of easy solution. For some time past a steam gunboat has been used as a tender to the School Ship, and serves to transport the Cadets back and forth; and it might even be that the old ship could have her bottom made flatter, so as to draw less water, in which case she could be moored close to the shore, and yet preserve all her imposing external appearance. She could be placed, let us say, quite near the entrance of the port, either on the Ninon side of the harbor, or on that of the new town, and then communication would be easy at all times.

If we pass now from the general system pursued at the School to the details of the course of instruction, we are at once struck with the great voids and superfluities existing therein, which, let us hope, may disappear in the re-organization which is now going on, thanks to our increased experience. In glancing over the list of studies pursued we are at first brought into contact with a complete course of French grammar and ethics.

Can it be credited, that after having required as a preliminary step to the admission of a Cadet, a perfect knowledge of composition and a Latin version of some French theme, it should be found requisite to send these young people to a " *Naval School*" to be instructed for an entire year in grammar, the rules of punctuation, and a knowledge of participles, to say nothing of a course of rhetoric! ! ! When this is done they pass to a course of universal history, in which the Navy (at least in former days) was completely overlooked.

In going through this course, some fifteen years ago one of the Professors was seized with an intense admiration for certain Albanian, Hungarian and Polish heroes, so that Scanderbeg, John Huniades and Podiebrad were, actually held up before the eyes of the Cadets as models for the imitation of officers of the French Navy, instead of such men as Duquesne, de Tourville and Suffren, who were never even so much as mentioned!

Since this ridiculous episode, Naval history has been made a part of the course, but it is even now taught by the Professor of Grammar, who passes without difficulty from a recitation upon the rules of Syntax, to the recital of famous naval battles, whilst at the same time there exists a course of Naval tactics which no one ever dreams of illustrating by a reference to our past maritime wars.

This same Professor is also obliged to instruct the Cadets in a course of geography which includes among other things, besides the grand divisions of the earth, such definitions as the word river, stream, island, peninsula, etc., etc., the rudiments of geology and physical geography, his duties terminating by a course of lectures on international law and maritime warfare and prize.*
All will allow, we think that this is a heavy imposition on the good nature of one man, and we very much question whether there are many college Professors in France willing to accept such a task as this.

In short, it is not possible to observe without amazement that the method of instruction so completely and

---

* Whilst the course of ethics alone occupies the first year of study, that of Universal and Naval history, physical geography, and maritime law divide between them the second year.

so well systematized in our military schools on shore is
here absurdly at fault.

When they leave the school, the Cadets are so completely ignorant of the Naval system of accounts, that
were it not for the presence on board ship of a Commissary they would not know that such a thing existed.*

It results, then, from this, that some of these young
men sometimes evince a great repugnance to perform
duty of this kind, frequently mingled with a sovereign
scorn for all persons and things connected with it, while
the greater number of them have not the faintest idea of
the manner in which a Navy is organized, clothed, equipped
or fed. Subsequently nevertheless, they become lieutenants and officers of divisions, and throw the burden of
their legitimate duties on the shoulders of the Commissary of the ship ; or if, as is sometimes the case, they
happen to sail with one of those rare commanders who
makes every one do his duty, and looks upon all this account
keeping as part of the profession, as much so indeed as
seamanship or gunnery, and who strictly requires his
subordinates to perform their share of such matters, they
are very much astonished, and believe they are degraded
by being called upon to perform such duties.

. While, still later, when these same young men become
Commanders, or executive officers, they know so little
about the matter as to be utterly unable to verify the
yeoman's accounts of the ship they command.

This is not, indeed, astonishing, and we ought not to

---

* In order to explain this it must be remembered that any officer in
the French Navy commanding a vessel with less than 100 men, may
be called upon to perform a Commissary's duty, and all commanding
officers are obliged to certify to the accuracy of the ship's accounts.—
Translator.

blame them for it, when we consider that the " Special Commission for improving Discipline, etc.," in drawing up a programme of studies for this School did not find it necessary to include in the course of instruction that which every Cadet should be absolutely obliged to *learn*.

All these deficiencies can, however, be remedied, and all defects easily corrected by suppressing certain branches now taught at the School which are absolutely useless, supplying their place with others more necessary, and making a good use of the steam gunboat we have referred to in order to teach upon a better plan those branches which by all means should be retained.

Already we find that a great improvement has taken place in the instruction in chemistry. In former years this branch was always taught on the School Ship, where there was neither laboratory nor proper materials for the subject, and where in consequence (at least some years since) the Professor's practical experiments failed about three-fourths of the time, amid the great applause and to the intense amusement of the Cadets.

At the present time the practical part of this branch is taught on shore, and a lecture room in the Naval Hospital devoted to the purpose.

In addition to these changes, the Infantry drills have been arranged upon a better footing, though the system is still capable of great improvement. Until last year these exercises for lack of room on shipboard were confined almost entirely to instruction in the Manual of Arms and the firings, while the midshipmen the moment they left the School for service afloat became, as is frequently the case in the Navy, victims of a system which without pre-vious teaching requires of them an unreasonable amount of information, being called upon to know not only the

School of the Company but the battalion drill, and obliged sometimes to command both.

This, however, is no longer the case, for now the Cadets are called upon to exercise in company and battalion drill on shore accompanied by artillery, to march and skirmish, to bivouac in advance and retreat, with pickets thrown out in the advance and rear, and the whole system is now regarded as an indispensable exercise and a salutary physical recreation.

But we will not fatigue our readers by pursuing this examination in detail. What we have already said will be quite enough to show that of all special military schools, .that of the Navy [the most difficult to systematize perfectly by reason of the extreme youth of the Cadets, and the wide range of information required of Naval officers] has remained up to this time the most thoroughly neglected.

A new system was commenced on the 1st of October, 1863, in a new School Ship, and the good results already attained thereby, lead us to hope that a new era is about to dawn upon this institution, and that the eye of the Minister of Marine once fixed steadily upon it, no means will be left untried to bring it to the greatest perfection possible. We may here add in a few words, that the principal changes required are a re-modelling of the entire programme of studies in such a way as to bring out in relief, as it were, the principles and elements of all the scientific branches taught; to add to every branch all the practical examples and illustrations it is possible to have suited to the eye and hand, for to see a thing once done practically, is worth ten times as much as an hour of verbal explanation. At the same time, such branches as shipbuilding, ordnance and Naval history, should be confided to men who have made a special study of the same;

in other words, who are themselves "experts," and who know, not merely the course required, but very much more.

This first task accomplished, there remains then, merely the recognition of this truth, that no system of study, not even the best that can be devised, will produce its full effect except in proportion as the Cadets bring a good disposition to their work and labor cheerfully and ambitiously. Let nothing, then, be neglected which may excite among them a generous emulation and desire to labor. Excite their self-love, their curiosity and their interest, and above all, do not forget to give them a full share of recreation and innocent amusement, for it cannot be too rigidly insisted upon that, so far from being injurious to study, these occasional distractions form the greater part of the success which invariably attends any good system of instruction.

In short, it is important that the Cadets should be trained as much as possible in an atmosphere of common sense and intelligence, in an atmosphere, moreover, impregnated with that spirit of ambition and patriotism which animates the service of which they are soon to become a part. Under this head much yet remains to be done, for up to the present moment literally nothing has been accomplished towards surrounding these young lads with the traditions of the Navy, and its brilliant souvenirs.

By all means, then, let these traditions and these souvenirs of the past be revived, not only in a lengthened course of Naval history, but as illustrative of the practice of gunnery, Naval construction, the defence of a coast line, dock-yard organization, the training of seamen, organization and equipment of distant expeditions for conquest or discovery, in which our Navy has borne so conspicuous a share. Everywhere let this appear, so that when some dead hero's name is mentioned, the instructor may be able to say, "This man whose name you now hear pronounced, has deserved well of his country, these are his deeds! these are the difficulties he surmounted and overcame! see what patience, what energy, what perseverance, what heroism, in short, he displayed! You have chosen to follow the same glorious vocation, and to become an inheritor of his fame. You are now of the same race, and he is now reckoned among your ancestors in glory. Never, then, forget that one day, perhaps, you may have the opportunity of imitating him; and labor now to the end that, when that glorious day comes, you may be worthy of him, indeed."

CHAPTER III.

A midshipman of the second class on leaving the "Borda" to commence his Naval career, has a good deal in common with those young fellows just quitting college, with their university honors fresh upon them; that is to say, he is very near to knowing a great many things, but as equally near to knowing nothing at all; * the more so, as from his debut he remains many months without putting into practice what he has learned. Generally speaking, even in the best disciplined vessels, we find too little attention paid to the instruction of those young men, or, with this object in view, any attempt to utilize the long sojourns in harbor or voyages at sea, even when there are on board of the vessel, officers who have ac-

---

* The best rendering of this passage is our English expression, "What he *thinks* he knows would fill a volume; what he does NOT know would fill a library."—*Translator.*

quired, by certain service, a special knowledge of important duties.

Those, for instance, who have served at the "experimental battery," or on the Gunnery Ships, and those who have been on detached service, whether in the batteries at Sebastopol, the expedition in China, Cochin China, or Mexico, (and these last are quite numerous at the present moment,) might easily instruct their younger comrades by means of lessons, from which they would derive much more profit than they do from waiting on a wharf until a late hour in the night, watching their boat's crew until their Captain returns from a ball, or the ward-room officers return from the theatre !

This service is, in truth, one of the last vestiges of certain ideas which pervaded the Service thirty years or more ago, and according to which it was believed to be a solemn duty to render a midshipman's life as hard and disagreeable as possible while trying to make a sailor of him. These were the good old days when quarantines were common, and midshipmen more often in arrest on the orlop deck, or perched upon a top-gallant yard to keep a sharp lookout for rocks, than promenading on shore; and when they oftener passed their nights by the light of the stars of heaven than in their hammocks.

In those days it was considered "the thing" to have tarry hands, a quid of tobacco always in the cheek, and to possess no more outfit than would fill a cocked hat box, to disdain, in short, whether far or near, all that which savored of luxury or comfort; and this feeling extended even to the affairs of the mess, if we may credit some of the officers of that day, who would have us believe that a midshipman's provision for a long cruise was neither extensive nor difficult to make. According to them, the steerage stores consisted of a sufficient number (more or less) of bottles of rum, and a couple of lean chickens, which, after having served to provide a mess of twelve midshipmen for a number of weeks, reached port hale and hearty after all ; the means taken to accomplish this wonderful feat being anything but miraculous. Every morning when the decks are washed, the chicken coops are placed on each side of the deck to be scrubbed also. Of course, it frequently happens that during this operation, some of the birds escape from the coop. The steerage boy was in those days required by the midshipmen to hold himself quietly in readiness near the coops, and whenever "a steerage chicken" was seen running about the decks, to catch it at once and place it in the steerage coop ; of course, all stray chickens were " steerage chickens;" and in this way the mess was always abundantly supplied, and no "INJUSTICE" done to anybody. This ingenious process, however, which no one ignored, and scarcely blamed, has of late years fallen into disuse in common with many other "good old practices ; " and for quite a number of years past, midshipmen have become civilized and respectable, in spite of the regrets they so frequently hear expressed around them by some of the older officers.

Those who have inaugurated this transformation, are to-day officers, and indeed such excellent officers, that they ought not to fear going much further in this way of progress and regulating or reshaping duty (on every occasion in which the discipline of the ship will not be injured thereby) to the profit and instruction of the midshipmen placed under their care, who will all reap the benefit of these reforms, though there are some that we will now advert to, who stand more particularly in need of just such advantages.

Every one knows that the Polytechnic School furnishes

a few scholars every year to the Navy.* Now, although
the special school of any service ought to be organized in
a way to give to the young people who enter it an education as conformable as possible to the requirements of
their future service, this arrangement, maintained simply
within its actual limits, could not, we believe, produce
always the best results, and at the present moment the
Navy owes to a wise departure from this system a certain number of its highest officers that it would not like
to see eliminated from its list. It is thus that some of
the members of this large body possess a very superior
mathematical education, which cannot, and in truth ought
not to be given at a Naval school—simply because such
knowledge is generally, and in fact practically useless to
the Cadets ; although in some rare cases it may render
great service.

It is true that Naval construction and ordnance which
play so important a part in our Naval system, number
among the sea officers [*i. e.*, Line officers] a certain number of followers who serve as a connecting link and bond
of union to the men who by different routes are all striv-
ing to attain the same end. A corps cannot, moreover,
isolate itself and repel all elements apparently foreign to
it, without exposing itself to the fate of some of those great
families we read of, who, by persisting for generations in
marrying only among themselves, have finally ended in
becoming perfectly and entirely exclusive—hated by their
neighbors and equals, and either idiotic or sterile.

Here again, as regards the Cadets who enter the Navy
from the Polytechnic, the principle is excellent, but the
same cannot be said of the result.

In truth, the Cadets intended for the Ordnance, Con-

---

* Eight entered the service last year.

struction, Engineering or Mining branches, before entering
their respective corps, pass a certain time, more or less
extended, in schools of instruction, but whether it is the
Navy is not regarded as a special service, or whether it is
that the Polytechnic School is looked on as a ship—
whose chimneys are masts, whose stairways are ratlins,
and whose dormitories are gun-decks, it is certain that
of all its Cadets those alone destined for the Navy are
deprived of the special preparation required, and launched
into their Naval career without any one seeming to care
for their instruction or being at all doubtful as to whether
or not they do not yet lack something under this head.

They become in a trice midshipmen of the first class,
that is to say, with rank of second lieutenants, and
although (as is sometimes the case) they may never have
put their foot on board ship, they are called upon on the
very first day they join their vessel to command the senior
midshipmen inured already to the Naval service, as well
as those of the second class, who alone have had three or
four years service afloat.

In face of a situation so mortifying to their self-respect,
as well as injurious to their future instruction, and the
discipline of the Service, they have no other course to
pursue than bravely to assume their duties among their
equals as well as inferiors in rank, and to learn their sea
duties by selecting a couple of good boatswain's mates,
and under their instruction learning to knot and splice,
and handle the great guns.   Still, after much hard labor,
they lack the knowledge of many things that they cannot
learn except by slow degrees in their service afloat, and
of which some of them remain for ever ignorant.   In a
word, those who possess sufficient moral courage to stoop
in order to learn, become good officers, but without ever
having been good practical sailors ; and this quality,

whose importance it is not necessary to exaggerate, is nevertheless exceedingly useful in the lower grades of the Service, where it always inspires the confidence and respect of the crew.

Whatever may be the motives alleged to justify an anomaly so strange, the true and only reason is probably that, owing to the small number of Cadets of this kind they have been overlooked, not having perhaps ever been thought of. It should have appeared and it does appear now very easy to send them on board of one of the drill corvettes at the Naval School for instruction in the practical parts of their profession, the time chosen being from the early part of August until the 20th of September, when the exercises are going on.

Associated during these two months with the Cadets of the "Borda," they would be the object of special care, and also able to make for themselves many friendships among their comrades of the future. They might after this receive their appointments, and, after two months' leave, they could report at Toulon, somewhat broken in to a sea-life, and in a condition to understand that which is constantly going on around them on shipboard. They should be embarked together for six months on board ship with officers specially designated to give them a course of practical instruction. They would thus pass through a regular school of practical instruction, and would no longer be subjected to the mortification of having to take charge of a watch without knowing either the method required or the orders necessary to work the vessel, or be obliged to place themselves under the tuition of their subordinates among the crew, when they are surrounded by their seniors, whose business and duty it is to instruct them. Such is, according to our view of the case, the true method of reaping all the benefit pos-

sible from the precious and hitherto too much neglected
material that the Polytechnic School sends every year
into the Navy.

We have now reached the lowest grade of commis-
sioned officer, and the Epaulette has replaced the "Ai-
guillette." The Ensign is theoretically qualified to the
charge of a ship; he is a fair sailor, but his experience
has not yet been great enough to allow his knowledge to
mature, as it will do in the future; in short, is more or
less incomplete in accordance with his opportunities for
service. Unfortunately, he is likely to remain a considerable time without the necessary experience required,
since no precaution is taken to assure for him, during
the first few years of his Naval life, that access to the two
great schools indispensable to the finishing of his education—distant ocean cruising, which makes the sailor;
and cruising in squadron, which makes the officer.

It must be allowed, however, that in such active times
as those we have had in the last ten years, it might be
difficult, if not impossible, to attain such results as we
would like to see attained. Under such a condition of
things, it is necessary for each man to outstrip experience by taking his own education in hand, and learning
as best he can, and how he can, his duties; but the active
service which we refer to is of itself a certain sort of
schooling, and has its own decided merit in forming
officers; but such stirring periods are not frequent, and
we can remember many long years of quiet and peace in
which three-fourths of our ships were laid up in ordinary,
and when the same officers made over and over again,
during their entire Naval career, the same cruises.

The great seaports on the Atlantic and Channel furnish ships for distant stations and ocean cruising, whilst
Toulon serves to fit out our squadrons and fleets, which

duty is always preferred by our Naval officers, and at-
tracts, little by little, to this port those officers who do
not care to stay at the others from family reasons, or
something of that nature. These latter ports, completely
stripped, are often obliged to require officers from
Toulon and the Mediterranean ports, which invariably
causes much trepidation among the officers located at
the latter. There was in such cases usually a general
scatter to the right and left ; the first officers in the
roster for duty, warned by their friends at headquarters
some little time beforehand, got out of the way in the
best way they could—one got leave, another a furlough,
another sick leave, a fourth some permanently "soft
billet ; " in short, when the fatal sea orders came, such
and such a man, who eight days before was tenth or
twelfth on the list for sea duty, found himself, to his
great astonishment and intense disgust, at the head of
the list, without there having been any apparent change
going on in the station. Of course good order and the
harmony of the Service was often rudely shaken by such
occurrences, and it in fact often happened that some
officers belonging to the ocean ports (i. e. Atlantic and
Channel ports) reached the grade of Post Captain without ever having been able, notwithstanding all their ex-
ertions, to serve in the fleet or squadron, while others
had never seen any other service, never having quitted
the Mediterranean.

Besides the measures necessary to complete the education of our young officers in varying their cruising
grounds, there are many others which, being susceptible
of immediate application, might all work towards the
same good result, and the omission of which it is difficult to explain. Such for instance are "Manuals of
Naval Practice," and " Aides-mémoires," which combine

in a portable and convenient form all the instruction
necessary in regard to the manifold details of the man-
agement and care of a vessel.   These are at the present
moment almost completely lacking, and the profession of
all others which exacts the greatest variety of information
is the only one it seems for which no one dreams of com-
posing a special book. Besides which, libraries to contain
technical works, voyages, and military histories, according to the available room on board, would offer a precious resource during long cruises at sea, without greatly
increasing the Naval budget of expense.

We may also mention as very much to be regretted the
absence of " general inspections," and of associations or
meetings among officers for improvement in professional
subjects.   Scattered over the four quarters of the globe,
they cannot, we admit, keep themselves constantly
posted in the improvements hourly going on at home,
and which, within the last few years, have changed so
completely the principles of maritime warfare in regard
to the attack and defence.   They cannot, in short, acquire
this information, unless while abroad they meet frequently among themselves to hear such subjects spoken
of and discussed by those recently from home.   These
conferences (simply good-humored talk among themselves), that commanding officers might in a thousand
ways render agreeable as well as useful both to themselves and their officers, would perfectly attain the end
we indicate.

As to the " general inspections," they ought to be made
as much as possible by Admirals specially charged with
this important duty; but in any case, and this is the
main point, they should bear not only on the good order,
drill, and discipline of ship and crew, but also upon the
degree of information and instruction of the officers of

the ship themselves, whose condition it is impossible to ascertain in any other way, and to this should be added a report as to the manner in which they understand and carry out the Regulations of the Navy. Is it necessary here to recall to the minds of our Naval readers how completely ignored or imperfectly known, prior to the year 1852, were those regulations even which had special reference to the officers themselves, and what a substantial benefit and boon was that little work in portable form,* which made its appearance about that time, and has since been within the reach of all?

These general inspections would make known at once the needs of this nature, and would furnish at the same time information as to the special labors of particular officers, and add reliable data upon which advancement in the service could be made which would have the effect of stimulating the zeal of others.

In the course of a long cruise many commanding officers carry out their instructions with a great degree of intelligence and ability in regard to reporting everything of interest to their Government which they may see on the voyage, but they forget much too often to associate their officers with them in these labors—those, at all events, who would be only too happy to second them in their task. Thanks to the customs of the service, thanks to the absence of official instruction on the subject, the greater number of our officers remain absolute strangers to the countries they visit. Hardly is the anchor down in a foreign port when they recommence a course (as equally monotonous and dull for them as for the crew) of the everlasting exercises required by the Routine Table. As to a verification of the charts, to a study of the mili-

---

* "Le Service interieur de la Marine Francaise," etc.

tary defences or fortifications of the harbor, of the resources of the port they are in, its facilities for repairing
or provisioning vessels, its productions, industries, commerce, or political condition, why, they might as well
have never heard of it, or visited it !

If they are anchored near some foreign ship of war, her
construction, rig, battery, engines, internal fittings, etc.,
whose examination would offer so much of interest and
instruction, pass equally unnoticed, while it would be so
very easy to have in the officers of every ship just as
many pairs of sharp, intelligent eyes open upon everything of interest which surrounds them, and as many
ready pens encouraged to make full reports (while labor-
ing for their own instruction) of all that their possessors
see in their incessant cruises around the world.

The complement of a vessel of war, as most persons know,
is composed of a Captain and a certain number of inferior
officers ; finally, of a Commissary and a Surgeon, and, although neither of these last-named may be educated for
Naval life, yet the duties they are called on to perform
are of such a nature, and so closely allied to the labors of
their Naval brethren, that we think our observations
would be incomplete if we passed on to the questions of
importance which still remain to be treated, without
glancing for a moment at the duties of the Commissary
and Surgeon.

The title of Commissary of a vessel of war is, perhaps,
the most ancient (if we except that of Admiral) known to
the French Navy ; but the original importance of the position has diminished little by little since the period of
the middle ages, until we find it as it exists in our day.
Placed originally upon the "Naves" that the king hired
to guard the interest of the crown and defend the sea-
coast, he was subsequently charged with the duty, not

only of overlooking the outlay and expenditure, but often of the conduct and character of his commander. He was charged with the duty of reporting to the High Stewards or Intendants of the realm the conduct of the Captain, both at sea and during an engagement ; and it was not without a long struggle, in which the most bitter animosity was shown, that these last finally obtained some modification of this state of things—so little in accordance with proper ideas of discipline. But this was at a period when the corps of officers was imperfectly organized, and when the responsibility which devolved on the commanders not being well guaranteed, the independence, more or less complete, of the accountant, seemed in truth the only safeguard of the king's treasury.

This necessity, of course, no longer exists in our day, and the Commissary is, at the present time, simply a member of the Council of Administration (i. e. Staff of the Captain), and charged with specific routine duties just as any other officer ; and, although often of the same rank, under the orders of the Commander.

The question has even arisen during the last few years as to whether it would not be advisable to pursue the same course as is adopted in the Army, and confide these duties to one of the officers of the Ship. This project, however, has few advocates and has encountered much opposition. It is alleged by Naval officers that the system of account-keeping and duties of Commissary are quite foreign to their tastes, their habits, and to their profession, already exacting such a variety of information on all subjects, when their position is compared with other military ones ; and, moreover, that they have little aptitude for "quill driving," as was amply shown in an unsuccessful attempt of this kind which took place during the Ministry of M. de Sartine.

We must own our belief, however, that these motives do not seem to us very conclusive. It would be easy to cite very many institutions or customs which are in full prosperity at the present time, which in former years were regarded as quite impracticable, or which absolutely failed, a century ago, and it is not a question at all of exacting additional knowledge of our officers, since they are already in many cases obliged, under their responsibilities, actual or pecuniary, to keep themselves wholly or partly familiar with accounts, so as to control the operations of the Commissary. In short, repugnance and lack of aptitude for this kind of duty seem to us to be more imaginary than real among them, and without looking very far away, we have in the English Navy a striking example of the little foundation for the greater part of the prejudices of this kind. The officers of the Royal Navy, for example, regard as secondary to their position and unworthy of their rank, the duties of the Master* (such as superintending the rigging of the ship and the care of the chronometers), that duty which with us is generally assigned as a special privilege to the officer chosen through the confidence of his Captain.

This singular prejudice of our British neighbors will certainly disappear on that day when the grade of Master (ricketty enough at this moment) is finally suppressed altogether, and this same effect will doubtless be produced among our Naval officers as soon as a new order of things in regard to matters of administration and accounts is established which may prove more in keeping with their true interests, and those of the Service. Is it not to be regretted, for example, when we see in certain difficult and painful emergencies of a cruise, two or three Ensigns

---

* Navigating Lieutenant,

or Lieutenants obliged to keep watch day and night and perform their drill duties besides, when in the same mess there is a Commissary whose whole business employs him not more than two or three hours in the twenty-four, and who cannot, no matter how willing he may be, give them the slightest relief ? Without alluding here to the many advantages which would result in employing for the "Administration" of line of battle ships and frigates, sea officers chosen by the Captain, who, with the assistance of the Staff of clerks and writers, would be perfectly equal to the task, and without crying out on principle for a measure of transformation so radical, we believe that at this moment, there would result manifest advantage to the service in replacing the Commissary on all ships not carrying armaments, by a sea officer, enjoying a small additional salary and doing his duty on deck at sea, while keeping the ship's accounts in port. In fact, when the Commissariat was reorganized lately, all Captains of vessels having less than 100 men, were saddled with the duties of Commissary in addition to those of their command. Whether we regard this as permanent or not, it is a step towards the system we have pointed out, but on principle, and as often as possible, according to our view, it should be one of the officers and not the Captain who should perform this duty.

We have simply a word to say in regard to the Surgeons. They are men who, having scarcely entered upon their professional career, and barely in possession of the very first elements of their medical education, are sent on shipboard. They pass their entire lives at sea ; the more they cruise the slower they advance, and they often undergo a lengthened period of sea service, enduring long and toilsome cruises, their chances for advancement to the summit of their profession growing fainter and fainter thereby. The highest position they can reach is that of a grade corresponding to "chef de bataillon," for the higher positions in the Navy being few, are reserved exclusively for the Professorships. This curious state of things arises from the fact that the special schools of medicine for the Navy exact of the personnel of the corps repeated competitive examinations, separated by long intervals of time and at particular periods.

A Naval surgeon, for example, in order to obtain a higher grade must prepare himself during his cruises at sea, and must be fortunate enough on his return home to arrive at the stated period for these examinations; if not, he may remain all his life in the third or second class, no matter what his services may have been, or however favorable the report of his superiors on shipboard. In consequence of the necessities of an active cruising life, these examinations fail in their object, and often present incredible inequalities to the detriment of the most meritorious men. But these inconveniences, already very serious, are as nothing when we consider the deplorable consequences this system entails upon the crews who are subjected to the treatment of incompetent persons. The Surgeons of the 3d class having little knowledge of their profession, and, above all, still less practice—since they are only beginners—are frequently embarked alone, and in the position of chief, on board of vessels having less than 45 men.

It would seem to follow then from this, that on board of these craft it is not allowable, under pain of being deprived of the doctor's care, to have more than a certain number [foreseen in advance] on the sick list, which is all the worse for those men who audaciously allow themselves to break through this rule, and have a greater number.

These extraordinary facts have been known to the service at large for a long time, and for a lengthened period many persons have sought for a means to remedy these evils; but it must be that the problem is a difficult one, since no person has yet been able to solve it satisfactorily. Nevertheless, a few weeks since there appeared an anonymous pamphlet, attributed to a gentleman high in authority in the medical department of the Navy, which at once drew public attention to these points we have alluded to, and some days after its appearance a Commission was appointed by the Minister of Marine to examine into the matter.

We are ignorant whether or not these two facts have any necessary connection between them, or whether, against all appearances, their succeeding each other at such a short interval is the simple effect of chance ; it is nevertheless, however, certain, according to our judgment, that the projects set forth in the said pamphlet contain the basis of a satisfactory solution which we may trust to see realized by success, judging from the vigor with which M. de Chasseloup-Laubat brushes away in his department the dust of superannuated customs.

According to the plan proposed, the competitive examinations, after being re-modelled, will no longer be held (outside of the Professorship) except for the two first grades or degrees, after which the medical career may be pursued freely up to the grade corresponding to that of Post Captain in the Navy, and all Surgeons embarked on shipboard, whether as chief or second, must have a doctor's diploma.

We have now gone over with our readers some of the most striking features of the shipboard existence of our Naval officers. Let us now rise a little in our position, and take a bird's-eye view of the entire service.

We see a re-union of men in which community of origin, labor, and existence strikingly dissimilar to all others, gives a character apart, a physiognomy, in short, strongly marked.　Nevertheless, and this is a singular feature: we have often heard the complaint, not without remonstrating against the exaggeration of such an opinion, that this élite body of men lacked unity, cohesion, or, to speak shortly, "esprit de corps."

We cannot believe that our Navy lacks "esprit de corps," and if any one will take into account the close relation brought about under the influence of daily needs and mutual supports, it will readily be seen that esprit de corps ought to be, and in fact is, stronger, more intelligent, and more elevated in the Navy than anywhere else.

But in order to acquire all its energy and all its lofty purity, this sentiment must rest upon the firm basis of the great and noble traditions of the past, of great and lofty aims and endeavors in the present and for the future.　Now in our Navy, these traditions which are as numerous as in other military bodies, are almost unknown, and there seems to exist no natural disposition to recall them or preserve them, while in our Army, the regiment is by its very perpetuity a faithful depository of its traditions, and as it were, an open book to be read by all, preserving by means of the men who succeed each other in its ranks from generation to generation, the immortal witnesses of its glorious actions in the past.

Without seeking, nevertheless [as many Ministers of Marine have uselessly attempted over and over again], to copy servilely an institution which cannot be adapted to its needs, the Navy also possesses its famous ships and the venerable names they bear.　Ships wear out, it is true, as do men themselves, and their existence is not as long even as that of the latter ; but their names never die,

at least never ought to be allowed to die. Have we not
yet a "Cordelière," a "Couronne," a "Belle-Poule," a
"Bretagne," a "Ville-de-Paris," and many others whose
predecessors were famous in different periods of the mon-
archy, whilst these same names are often only so many
dead letters, so frequently is it the case that the officers
on board of the ships which bear them are utterly ignorant of their previous history.

Now this is all wrong ; these traditions should be ex-
plained and revived ; it would animate the service as
if with a new life. Every ship of war which has a
history should preserve it, not solely in the archives of
the Minister of Marine [which is no great thing after all],
but on board, and her history should be in three parts—a
detailed account of all her services and the battles she
had been engaged in, a roll of honor, or summary of the
same; finally, a plate of copper should be engraved with
her history, and fastened over the wheel at the break of
the poop, while another should be attached to the main-
mast, so that every man in the ship should know the
vessel's history.

No page, no line should ever be added to this without
the consent of the Board of Admiralty, and this triple
history should carefully be preserved, and, when the vessel is laid up in ordinary or disarmed, carefully deposited
at the "Prefecture Maritime."

We are convinced that every officer in the Navy would
hail this innovation with satisfaction, and although it is
apparently an insignificant thing in appearance, it would
not be long without exercising a most happy influence
upon the minds, even of the crew ; for if men do exist
(and we admit there are many) who have no need of the
examples of the past to nerve them to the accomplishment
of prodigies of devotion and valor, yet even these, and

with very much stronger reasons, all others may find that there is nothing like that sentiment which is inspired by being surrounded with the memorials of time-honored and noble souvenirs.

So much, then, for the traditions of the past ; let us take a look at the labors of the present and the future.

These labors are so widely scattered over all the points of the globe, both habited and uninhabited, and are so numerous, that, in fact, a few years ago our officers could not obtain the smallest leave of absence in order to enjoy that repose so indispensable after the fatigues of long and exhausting cruises, and were not numerous enough to supply even the actual demands of the service, daily increasing.* It was, therefore, necessary to increase the number in the grades, a measure always popular, but only advantageous for a corps when brought about by a need permanent and real, since, if otherwise, it exposes them to the painful necessity of an ultimate reduction. In reality, however, it was not the Crimean war, nor the Italian war, nor the wars in China and Cochin-China, nor the land expeditions sent into Italy and Mexico, which necessitated the increase of the personnel of the service, but the introduction of a system entirely novel, in short, worthy to be termed from the proportions it has assumed within the past ten years—a powerful " transport Navy."

Before the Crimean war the transport fleet numbered only thirty-two (32) sailing vessels, of an aggregate tonnage of 15,550 tons, and requiring to man them 2,000 men and 150 officers, some of these ships being armed or employed as School ships, whilst others had no more than a single officer, or perhaps a pilot, on board. At this

---

* Report of Minister of Marine to the Emperor.

moment, however, we posses 75 transports, of which 43 are steamers, aggregating a total tonnage of 60,000, and requiring a personnel of 7,000 persons, of which 400 are officers, and in this imposing list are not included at all those line-of-battle ships, frigates and corvettes which have frequently been similarly employed.

It would seem, then, from the data which are furnished by official documents disseminated through divers publications which we have at present before our eyes, that of 1,000 subaltern officers, such as Lieutenants and Ensigns, embarked on shipboard during the last four years, 400 or 500 at least (the figures are rather below than above the truth) have been employed in the transport fleet.* This fact explains at once, very naturally, the necessity for increasing the number of officers in the several grades.

But beyond this the fact has sufficient importance of itself to arrest our attention for the moment, while we examine a little closer into the probable consequences.

In a material point of view, this new fleet is considered as an indispensable addition to our military power as a means of quickly mobilizing our Army and of striking decisive blows by throwing a force suddenly and without warning beyond the seas. That would be, of course, a result of which no one would dispute the advantages, but in looking at the matter a little closer, we perceive that of the three elements which compose an army, viz.: men, horses,

---

* England possesses, at the present moment, 21 transports, of which 11 are commanded by Masters. The other 10 employ 25 Lieutenants out of a total of 627 Lieutenants and Sub-Lieutenants actually on sea service. It is easy to see what a tremendous difference there is between these figures and those we have given above for France.

Englishmen have always been zealous, perhaps to an excessive degree, of preserving to their officers a character purely and wholly military.

materiel and provisions, the second alone exacts for its
transportation a special kind of vessel ; for experience
has proved that, in order to transport men, there is nothing like a fleet of ships armed " en flûte".* (*i. e.*, with spar
deck guns only), and all merchant ships are able to carry
equipments, stores, and provisions. The transports especially for horses are those alone which it is necessary
to have, but even for these it is necessary to avoid
running into extremes, since after having constructed
them, some authorities may wish to make use of them,
and for lack of horses to transport employ them in carrying materiel, which would be a ruinous piece of economy
for the Government, which sails its vessels much more ex-
pensively than merchants do, and employs twice or three
times as many persons to do exactly the same work.
Moreover, this plan would be detrimental to commerce,
which finds its profits in such charters, of which it would
thus be deprived, as well as injurious to the sailors themselves, who are always better paid when working for private companies or individuals. This ruinous economy,
we say, has not been spared us in the last four years, if
we may judge by the figures we have given, and, above
all, it has had the effect of turning a considerable number
of officers away from their legitimate duties, causing them
to lose their military habits and ideas of discipline, and
obliterating from their memory a multitude of professional details. On board of a transport, it is true that an
officer is practised in navigation and seamanship, but it is
not in the actual circumstances that we may fear for him

---

* Of course it will be understood here that it is not a question of
embarking troops upon ships of war exposed to the chances of battle.
That system, essentially bad, has long since been condemned, and no
one dreams of reviving it.

the lack of this knowledge. Beyond this his work con-
sists solely in embarking and disembarking men and
packagés, stowing both so as to occupy as little space as
possible, and in organizing the men's mess and steward's
arrangement for the table of the officers who may be pas-
sengers. This last duty is not the least difficult by any
means, and is, as a rule, so apt to compromise the officers'
dignity that it is much to be desired that the Department
of Marine would establish victualling contractors on board
of transports to remedy the inconveniences of the present
regime.

In face of these multiplied occupations, it is no longer
a question with these officers, either of the discipline and
cleanliness of their ship or of the instruction of the men,
to the very great detriment of the military regularity requisite in the Navy, and it frequently happens that after
two, four, or even ten years of such duties, the officer
finds himself unexpectedly on board a regular man-of-
war either as officer of the watch, divisional officer, or
ordnance officer of an iron-clad. He is thus suddenly
called upon to perform his legitimate duties, and finds
himself no longer able to do so efficiently, owing to the
changes which have taken place during his absençe in
" transport service." Whether it be the improvements in
construction, ordnance, or material of war, he is ignorant
of them all, and while he is hard at work studying to re-
gain what he has lost, another officer takes his place in
the transport service, to forget also all that he has ac-
quired in the performance of his proper duties.

This is a true picture of what has been going on in the
Navy lately, and it would seem to be of a nature to cause
us reflection, since we desire to have a Navy for purposes
of war, and we spend every year for this object 125 mil-
lions ($25,000,000), but if we do not take care we risk

the chance of being greatly deceived at some moment.
If the Minister of War, for instance, employed half his
cavalry force in continually guarding wagon trains, he
would hardly expect after twenty years of such service to
find his cavalry fit for their regular duties, or imagine he
had a cavalry force for combat ; why then should similar
causes have a different effect on the Navy ?   Let us take
courage and look this new danger in the face, and see
what can be done to remedy these evils.   Do we wish absolutely to keep up the transport service or increase the
number of these vessels ?   Then there should be no hesi-
tation, no halting between opinions, but a corps of special officers for this service should at once be created,
either as auxiliary, if the command of these ships is reserved to Naval officers, or on half-pay if one prefers
(after a plan too long to be discussed here) to form for
the ordinary duties of this service a nucleus of officers
coming from the Naval School, and advancing by themselves from the grade of Ensign to that of a flag officer,
in which case they would not be distinguishable from
their comrades except by the diversity of their duties.

But better than all, according to our view, is to stop
at once and not proceed any farther in this matter, leaving to the merchant marine and the Navy the rôle which
belongs to each naturally.   Leave to the merchant captain the care of transporting to all quarters of the globe
the products of our industry, both material and agricul-
tural,—to render, in short, all the service which may be
the object of direct remuneration, since in performing
this task while enriching himself he enriches his country.

On the other hand, leave to the Naval officer the care
of showing our flag everywhere, of protecting our commerce, of undertaking for its benefit those distant surveying
expeditions which open up new routes through distant seas.

To him belongs the honor of being the shield of France upon the ocean.   He alone has the glory of defending its coasts, sword in hand, and striking from afar all who may attack his flag, or who fail to respect it.   This task is certainly sufficiently grand, sufficiently noble and vast, to prevent his being diverted from it by occupations for-, eign to the profession, at the risk of altering the character and tone of the entire corps of officers, and of causing a festering wound in the service, it may be difficult, if not impossible, to heal,--at the risk, in short, of discovering, perhaps too late, on the eve of a great maritime war, that we possess, indeed, ships, steamships, cuirassed ships, ships to go under water, over water, and perhaps even through the air, but that we have no longer any officers.

We fear that even the limited number we now have are gradually disappearing little by little, and are not being replaced, as was the case in former years, while the young men throughout the country, who are drawn by their inclinations to the profession of arms, no longer dream of entering the Navy.   This effect is already seen in a most striking way, for at the competitive examinations of the last dozen years more than 500 young men annually disputed for the positions of Cadets at the Naval School, while within the last four years the number has been only from 250 to 330, and it will be in vain, in our opinion, that the authorities seek a remedy for this falling off in increasing the grades, in special promotions, in decorations, in any favors of any kind ; the human heart has higher needs than the mere bestowal of trifles.   Let skeptical moralists reason at random upon the progressive decadence of humanity, and complain of the self-interest and egotism which, according to their notions, pervades this age, we will not oppose them, but we, who are aiming at a practical result, remember that it is even now as was the case eighteen hundred years ago, that " man does not live by bread alone," and that until the termination of the world, the only means of creating a corps of intelligent, educated men, ready at all times to devote their lives to the service of their country, is to hold out to them noble duties to perform, labors to undergo, difficulties to conquer, while exacting of them the high qualifications required of them in their profession.   Give them, then, position, advantages, and suitable rewards—that is only justice pure and simple; but let us not be seduced into the belief that we have done everything required, because we have given them ribbons for their button-holes, embroidery for their coats, or sprinkled a few stars here and there on the crests of their epaulettes.

VALUABLE WORKS

ON

Naval Science and Naval Engineering.

PUBLISHED BY

D. VAN NOSTRAND,

23 Murray and 27 Warren Street, New York.

LUCE'S SEAMANSHIP: Compiled from various authorities and illustrated with numerous original and select designs. For the use of the United States Naval Academy. By S. B. Luce, Lieutenant Commander, U. S. Navy. Fourth edition, revised and improved. Crown octavo, half roan, $7.50.

MODERN MARINE ENGINEERING, Applied to Paddle and Screw Propulsion. Consisting of 36 Colored Plates, and 259 Practical Woodcut Illustrations, and 403 pages of Descriptive Matter, the whole being an exposition of the present practice of the following firms: Messrs. I. Penn & Sons, Messrs. Maudslay, Sons & Co., Messrs. James Watt & Co., Messrs. T. & J. Rennie, Messrs. R. Napier & Son, and other prominent Builders. One vol., 4to, cloth, $25.00; half-morocco, $30.00.

NAVAL DRY DOCKS OF THE UNITED STATES. By General C. B. Stuart. Illustrated with twenty-five fine engravings on steel. Fourth edition, 4to, cloth, $6.00

SUBMARINE WARFARE, DEFENSIVE AND OFFENSIVE. Comprising a full and complete History of the invention of the Torpedo, its employment in War, and results of its use. Descriptions of the various forms of Torpedoes, Submarine Batteries and Torpedo Boats actually used in War. Methods of ignition by Machinery, Contact Fuzes, and Electricity, and a full account of experiments made to determine the Explosive Force of Gunpowder under Water. Also a discussion of the offensive Torpedo system, its effect upon Iron-Clad Ship systems, and influence upon Future Naval Wars. By Lieut.-Commander John S. Barnes, U. S. N. With illustrations. 1 vol., 8vo, cloth, $5.00.

METHOD OF COMPARING THE LINES AND DRAUGHT-ING VESSELS, Propelled by Sail or Steam, including a chapter on Laying off on the Mould Loft Floor. By Samuel M. Pook, Naval Constructor. With illustrations, 8vo, cloth, $5.00.

SLIDE VALVE AND LINK MOTION, To Stationary, Portable, Locomotive, and Marine Engineering; with new and simple methods for proportioning the parts. By W. S. Auchincloss, C. E. Illustrated with 37 Woodcuts and 21 Lithographic Plates, together with a Travel Scale and numerous Useful Tables. Third edition, 8vo, cloth, $3.00.

NAVIGATION AND NAUTICAL ASTRONOMY: Prepared for the use of the United States Naval Academy. By Prof. J. H. C. COFFIN. Fourth edition, enlarged, 12mo., cloth, $3.50.

THEORETICAL NAVIGATION AND NAUTICAL ASTRONOMY. By LEWIS CLARK, Lieut. Commander U. S. N. Illustrated, 8vo, cloth, $3.00.

THE STEAM ENGINE INDICATOR, and the Improved Manometer Steam and Vacuum Gauges: Their Utility and Application. By PAUL STILLMAN. New edition, 12mo, cloth, $1.00.

NAUTICAL ROUTINE AND STOWAGE, with Short Rules in Navigation. By JOHN MCLEOD MURPHY and WM. N. JEFFERS, Jr., U. S. N. 1 vol., 8vo, cloth, $2.50.

LESSONS AND PRACTICAL NOTES ON STEAM, the Steam Engine, Propellers, etc., etc. For Young Marine Engineers, Students and others. By the late W. R. KING, U. S. N. Revised by Chief-Engineer J. W. KING, U. S. N. Twelfth edition, 8vo, cloth, $2.00.

A TREATISE ON THE RICHARDS STEAM ENGINE INDICATOR, with Directions for its use. By CHARLES T. PORTER. Revised, with Notes and Large Additions, as developed by American Practice; with an Appendix, containing Useful Formulæ and Rules for Engineers. By F. W. BACON. 12mo, illustrated; cloth, $1.00.

TREATISE ON NAUTICAL SURVEYING. By Capt. W. N. JEFFERS, U. S. N. Illustrated; 8vo, cloth, $5.00.

A TREATISE ON ORDNANCE AND NAVAL GUNNERY: Compiled and arranged as a Text Book for the U. S. Naval Academy. By Commander EDWARD SIMPSON, U. S. N. Illustrated with 185 engravings, 8vo, cloth, $5.00

SQUADRON TACTICS UNDER STEAM. By FOXHALL A. PARKER, Captain U. S. Navy. Published by authority of the Navy Department. Illustrated with 77 Plates, 8vo, cloth, $5.00.

FLEET TACTICS UNDER STEAM. By FOXHALL A. PARKER, Captain U. S. Navy. Illustrated by 140 Woodcuts, 18mo., cloth, $2.50.

GUNNERY CATECHISM, as applied to the Service of Naval Ordnance. Adapted to the latest Official Regulations, and approved by the Bureau of Ordnance, Navy Department. By J. D. BRANDT, formerly of the U. S. Navy. Revised edition, illustrated, 18mo., cloth, $1.50.

ORDNANCE INSTRUCTIONS FOR THE UNITED STATES NAVY. Part I. Relating to the Preparation of Vessels of War for Battle, and to the Duties of Officers, and others when at Quarters. Part II. The Equipment and Manœuvre of Boats, and Exercise of Howitzers. Part III. Ordnance and Ordnance Stores. Published by order of the Navy Department. Illustrated. 8vo, cloth, $5.00.

NAVAL DUTIES AND DISCIPLINE: With the Policy and Principles of Naval Organization. By F. A. ROE, Late Commander, U. S. Navy. 12mo, cloth, $1.50.

THE RECORDS OF LIVING OFFICERS of the U. S. Navy and Marine Corps. Compiled from official sources. By LEWIS B. HAMERSLY, Late Lieutenant, U. S. Marine Corps. Revised Edition. 8vo, cloth, $5.00.

www.ingramcontent.com/pod-product-compliance
Lightning Source LLC
Chambersburg PA
CBHW021634270326
41931CB00008B/1022